GET TO LEVEL NEXT

Find your life changing moment

notionpress
.com

GET TO LEVEL NEXT

Find your life changing moment

BENNY GEORGE

notionpress.com

Notion Press

Old No. 38, New No. 6

McNichols Road, Chetpet

Chennai - 600 031

First Published by Notion Press 2016

ISBN 978-93-5206-996-5

Dedication

To my love, Sarah who stands by me and continues to believe in me and to my daughter, Alina who makes my life meaningful.

Contents

Foreword

Oxford Dictionary defines "success" as

1) accomplishment of aim or purpose and 2) the attainment of name, fame and social status. However, in real life the term success is not easy to define as it indicates something that goes beyond achieving goals or attaining fame and social status. Success in life invariably refers to leading a happy and productive life, tackling the challenges on the professional and personal fronts with poise, while being able to contribute to the society in a positive manner. This, in turn, requires a person to have a balanced approach towards life, capable of taking in the rough with the smooth without allowing the thrills, joys, despondencies and sorrows to affect him unduly. In other words, development of a proper personality with a positive attitude is the key to achieving success in life.

Benny George, my contemporary during school days, has penned this work on how improvement of one's personality and attitude towards life involves taking a series of small measures which can be accomplished by everyone who sets his heart and soul into this effort. He has put it across very succinctly that success involves a series of steps, each aimed at taking the pursuer to the next higher level. It is a continuous process of learning and self improvement which never stops; with each successful step the goal gets shifted to the next higher level. He has outlined the importance of cultivating good habits, living in harmony with human beings as well as with nature, possessing an open mind that would absorb the good, while weeding out the bad and developing a sensitive mind. He defines excellence in simple words as an attitude that does not allow one to settle for mediocrity and emphasises the importance of listening in communication.

One trait that is found in most individuals who settle for a life of mediocrity, despite being blessed with copious amounts of talent and ability, is their tendency to live within their personal comfort zone. Lives of great men teach us the fact that they could reach the heights they did only because they were willing to break out of their comfort zones and venture into unknown territories. The challenges and difficulties thrown up helped them to sharpen their skills and bring the best out of them by pushing their limits. The words

"heights that great men reached were not achieved by a single flight,

they, while their companions slept were toiling upwards in the night"

convey the secret of success in cryptic words. Benny has elaborated on this and explained that "toiling" involves, in addition to hard work, resilience, tenacity, ability to manage time and effective use of technology.

A message that comes out of each page of this book is the need to give back to society at every step. We tend to take many of the things around us for granted; if we pause and think how life would be without any of those things we would understand their importance in making us what we are. The world we are living in is an intensely competitive one; however, that does not indicate that one should surrender the capacity to understand, empathise and help those who need ones time and assistance. The good will earned by such acts would more than make up the small material losses that might occur while performing them.

Benny George has written this book based on the experience he has gained by working for nearly two decades in this field. Written in simple language using elegant prose and peppered with numerous examples, this book is an easy read devoid of management and technical jargon that one tends to find in most of the other books of this genre. This book should be read by all those who wish to go forward in life. I wish the book and its author all success.

– Dr. K.N. Raghavan IRS

Acknowledgement

This book has been a long awaited dream come true. I am thankful to God Almighty for giving me the energy and the countless resources to make my dream come true. My heart is filled with gratitude to all my teachers at different stages of my life, who gave me priceless lessons which has guided my thought processes throughout the making of this book. I am grateful to my parents who gave me the first lesson in being human and taught me that I should always take the next step. I wish to thank Sumi Thomas of DropCap Media, who patiently edited this work and gave it proper shape. I would also like to remember with gratitude Vikram Dhar, my Coach, who gave me the realisation that I can move to the next level. I acknowledge the inspiration of all the participants of all my training programs who lifted my spirits and made me aware that I can contribute. And finally I thank the authors of all the books that I read, which contributed immensely in shaping my thinking.

Introduction

Every day is the beginning of the rest of your life. Each new dawn brings with it new hopes and opportunities. And life beckons, waiting to be celebrated. With this awareness, let us start a movement to co-exist in harmony and mutual respect; make a promise of not hurting anyone: comply and co-exist!

The word harmony in effect means "a pleasing combination of elements in a whole." The key word here is "pleasing." In a community, there is harmony when people are nice to one another and when people get along together. For that to happen, we must learn to accept others unconditionally. Give everybody space and time.

Compliance with basic societal and civic guidelines result in a better-behaved person. Mutual respect and tolerance reduce instances of flaring tempers and knee-jerk reactions. This eventually leads to more peaceful co-existence and harmonious interaction among people. Let us learn to combine happiness and healthy relationships; let us create harmony.

Children learn everything from their elders. They do not go by what elders tell them to do, but they watch instead. They are constant observers of their parents, teachers and other elders around them and take cues from all that they see. Can we make an effort to be compliant citizens and thus help the next generation also be compliant? Can we show them that we respect each other everywhere so that they also learn to respect each other? Let us bring up a new generation that will comply and co-exist by learning from example.

Chapter 1

Living Mindfully

I recently came upon this quote: "Man can live about 40 days without food, about three days without water, about eight minutes without air... but only for one second without hope." Indeed, when hope dies, the spirit dies.

Hope is nothing but your aspirations for your family, your society and your country at large. Willingness to transform these hopes into actions produces exciting outcomes that lift your spirit and spur you on into further action. You then start activating people around you with the same spirit and the entire community moves forward with a synergistic spirit that can never be stopped! This is where the magic begins. Each moment of hope spreads positive vibes and brings people together.

Staying Positive

Sir Winston Churchill once said, "The empires of the future are the empires of the mind." Many of us do not realise the power of the mind. The mind is capable of creating what we ask it to create. The sad part is that a majority of us keep telling our minds about things that we do not want or things that do not bring any happiness in our lives.

Here is an example: Imagine we fall sick and are admitted to a hospital. To our visitors, we narrate our story of illness, all that the family is having to put up with because of the hospitalisation and the financial burden that comes with it—the list of laments is unending. But pause for a moment and ask yourself, "Is this what I want?" I am sure it is not! So think and talk about how much better you feel after getting medical care and about being able to go back home soon. This way, you bring positivity. The result is that you actually feel better and heal faster. Try it, you could actually create an empire of positivity for yourself!

Gratitude goes a long way in building a positive attitude. Learning to count our blessings in life is of paramount importance. However, a vast majority of us are busy worrying about what we do not have. Once we start counting our blessings, then we would only have time to thank God. The very fact that I am able to write my thoughts and you are able to read it is good enough for us to be grateful. Hey, we are alive today!

Let us make an effort to look at what we have and be thankful.

Another important positive attribute is that of modesty. Humility helps us have a "teachable attitude." It allows you to observe and make every moment a learning experience. Humility and pride do not co-exist. The day you feel that you have learned everything, you cease to be alive. Everybody around us can teach us something, the value of which may not be obvious at that point in time. It may come in handy when you least expect it. Let us work hard to be humble and stay lifelong students.

Sensitivity

"When I do good, I feel good; when I do bad, I feel bad, and that is my religion"—well-spoken words by Abraham Lincoln and ever so true. Very relevant for the 21st century too. Here is a question to ponder upon: Do we really "feel" any feeling, or have we become immune to feelings? I think we have become immune. Simply put, we do not care anymore.

Even if we do, the line between "good feeling" and "bad feeling" is so blurred that we just do what we like to do, without thinking about how it makes us feel. We seem mostly unconcerned about how it impacts others.

Take for instance, how people get into arguments. They lash back and forth, becoming louder by the minute, neither side showing willingness to listen.

Finally the winner emerges with a triumphant grin. Does this sound familiar? The fact is that the people who are involved in an argument hardly hear the other person. They spend a considerable amount of time, words and energy till one of them out-shouts the other and becomes a self-declared winner. What would the real outcome of such arguments be? Remember this throughout your life: "You may win an argument, but you would have lost the person!"

In short, we have lost our sensitivity. We are only sensitive about ourselves and our benefits. Can we put in some effort to develop a sensitive heart, which takes others also into consideration before doing something? Let us try and do those things that make us feel good and avoid those that would not.

Overcoming Negativity

There is the well-told story of Bucephalus, the famous horse of Alexander the Great. It is said that King Philip II, Alexander's father, was not interested in this horse as it had not been possible to tame him—the horse would not let anyone mount him. Alexander decided to try taming the creature. He understood why the horse was irritated. He spoke soothingly to the horse and turned it towards the sun so that it could no longer see its own shadow, which was making him skittish.

In more modern times, we had Helen Keller who said, "Keep your face to the sunshine and you cannot see a shadow." When pains and burdens cast shadows in our lives, we tend to get irritated, depressed and angry at things around us. We fail to see the brighter side of life. Turn your face to the sunshine—the blessings in your life—and there will be no more shadows disturbing you. You will become calm and peaceful. You would then, like Bucephalus and Alexander, conquer the world, your world!

Open Your Mind

Being true to yourself is crucial for inner growth. "If you cannot handle the answer, do not ask the question." What an insightful statement! Many a time, we ask questions expecting a certain answer. When we have to face an answer that we cannot accept, we flounder. In any situation, we should prepare ourselves to handle the outcome regardless of whether it is favourable or unfavourable. Asking a question with an open mind is the key!

Basketball ace Michael Jordan once said, "I have failed over and over and over again in my life and that is why I succeed." We give up on ourselves on many occasions and call ourselves failures. We introspect and talk to others, highlighting the failures that we have gone through. We conclude saying, "I am good for nothing."

The age-old saying might say this: "Failure is the stepping stone to success." However, I will not tell you that. What I want you to internalise is that you failed in one attempt towards what you wanted to do.

You have many more attempts left. But you will fail when you stop attempting. Keep trying with renewed focus, vigour and enthusiasm and then success cannot help but present itself to you. You have been created to win!

The path to winning starts when you start living your life in every moment. We all get beautiful gifts on special occasions like birthdays and anniversaries. What do you do with yours? If you are like most people, those special gifts would be safely put away (far from children's reach probably) for a special occasion. Am I right? What do you do with the best outfit that you own? Keep it safe and neat to be worn on a special day, when it comes. What do you do with those expensive plates and cutlery? Store it in the well-lit cupboard in your dining room. Am I right again? When are you going to use all that? When is that special occasion? Whom are you waiting for to come and admire you wearing that beautiful dress? Let me look you straight in the eye and tell you: Burn those aromatic candles, wear that nice dress and use those expensive plates! Do not save it for a special day, because today is special!

I read some time ago that "when little people try to drive you down, think big." Yes, there are people who want you to lose or who wish that misfortune finds you. However, if you learn to think big, you will be immune to the attacks of petty people. On the other hand, when you fight petty people, you reduce yourself to their size. Their attacks are proof enough that you are growing. If you start thinking big, you will only feel sorry for such people. So, stay big. Give way to small people who race against you and let them win. Your aim is far greater. Stay focussed on those goals and do not let the distractions bother you. Remember, you are a unique creation of God, destined to do big things!

You are What You Think

At the end of a bad day, a day when deadlines were missed, targets were not achieved and appointments cancelled, most of us say to ourselves, "When I woke up today, I knew that it was going to be a bad day." If you knew that, what effort did you put in to make it good? Why did you not change your thinking to "it is going to be a GREAT day"? My firm belief is that our thinking is what makes the day good or bad. What we think in our minds is what happens in our lives. Thus, if you want to change the way you live, change the way you think. Think you are a winner and you definitely will be!

"If you think you can, you can. If you think you can't, you can't. Either way you're right." Not my words, but American industrialist and innovator Henry Ford's. How true! Many of us walk the face of this earth with self-demeaning thoughts and blame everything around us for all the problems that we face. All those limiting thoughts may actually come true as that is what your mind believes. Get out of that negativity. Think "I can" and you will! There are things only you can do, and those things are waiting for you.

What is the right path towards larger goals? How do we resolve the obstacles that crop up on our way? You have surely heard of out-of-the-box thinking. It urges you to think unconventionally. It is said that thinking out of the box will help generate new ideas and new approaches. I would like to apply this concept to problem solving. Think out-of-the-problem!

Conventionally, you are inclined to search for solutions by digging deeper into the problem itself, producing a quicksand effect—you just keep sinking more. Instead, look at the problem from different angles as if you are an outsider. You will be amazed at the possibilities that this could throw up. When you do this, you are detaching yourself from the problem and forcing yourself to think from the outside.

Tackling Success

Excellence is an attitude that requires you to put in more than 100 per cent in everything you do. It is about refusing to take short cuts and hitting the target that you set for yourself every time, about the willingness to run that extra mile. It pushes you to the next level of performance. Excellence is seen in small details of the big picture. It does not allow you to settle for mediocrity. When you exhibit excellence, you pull others also onto that platform and the result is extraordinary.

Yes, we also need to reach out to others on our path to success in life. Effective communication does not happen when the message goes from one's brain to the other's brain. It happens when the message goes from one's heart to others' hearts. And that is why we talk about "heart to heart" conversations. Let us work towards employing our hearts more and let us feel the change!

Communication is essentially about the willingness to listen. Unfortunately, the ability to communicate is most often measured by the way one talks, presents or writes with an ability to convince receivers. Thus, all of us strive to be effective talkers and the importance of listening is undermined. "LISTEN" when rearranged becomes "SILENT." To be a good listener, one has to be silent and focus on what is being said. Listen to understand and not to reply. Yes, it takes a lot of effort, but it is an effort worth taking.

This is one of the most beautiful sentences I have ever read: "You can either have my sympathy or my respect. You cannot have both." The world respects people who fight adverse circumstances. Winning is not as important as the willingness to fight. However, whining about adversities makes you a victim. Be willing to take adversities head on. It makes you stronger and more confident.

Baggage of the Past

One thing we need to be wary of on our path to success is the baggage of the past. When we are travelling, the weight of our luggage determines the pace of our movement forward. This is true in life as well. If we are carrying along our bad experiences from the past, we tend to be sluggish. We think more about what went wrong with our lives than what we did right. We think about the failures that we had to face more than the little victories. We think more about how much we were hurt by others than the occasions when we were helped by many.

We lug such limiting thoughts along until they become a heavy burden on our shoulders. This burden impedes our progress in life. Can we make an effort to put down these burdens, look forward and take determined strides that will get us closer to our goals?

The Way Forward

Confidence is the courage to take action even when you are weighed down with fear. Confidence is not the absence of fear, but the willingness to look fear in the eye. You have to get out of your comfort zone to develop confidence. You also draw strength from your past experiences. When you act with confidence, you become magnetic and attract positive energy to make things happen for you.

Enthusiasm is the key to good performance and superb results. Begin your day with gusto and you will experience the rush of adrenaline in your system. Not just that—enthusiasm is contagious! It spreads fast and spurs others on into the action zone. It is character-based and not context-driven. It is said that "everybody lights up a room—some when they walk in, and some when they walk out." Which group would you want to belong to? I believe you should belong to the first group. Let us make an effort to be enthusiastic and light up not just rooms, but as many hearts as possible!

Persistence pays. I read somewhere that in the continuing fight between water and rock, as on a rocky seashore, it is water that ultimately wins, creating a beautiful beach. It is not always the force of the water that polishes the rock, but the time that it spends washing over it. Persistent effort in achieving something that you have set your heart to will definitely produce results. Like the villagers in the story who used to sing and dance to please the rain gods (for the full story, go to the chapter "*Living for others: Giving back to society*"), are you willing to dance till it rains or will you dance for some time and wait for the rains? I trust you will keep at it till it rains!

A doctor once told me the story of a young widow with two children aged 4 and 1, who came to consult with him. She was diagnosed with breast cancer and was told that she might just have another six months to live. She refused to accept this, saying she had a lot of work to do bringing up her children, educating them and getting them on their feet. She refused to stay in the hospital for a long time saying her children needed her and wanted the doctor to finish treatment as soon as possible. And guess what? She lived on to bring up the children and is now bringing up her grandchildren as well! Do you have that kind of fight in you?

For many of us, "happiness" is a conditional occurrence. We say that we will be happy if this happens, or if we achieve that in life, or if something or the other comes our way, and so on. Thus, we submit so much to different situations and allow situations to dictate terms about our own happiness. Is that fair? I believe a happy person is someone with a certain set of attitudes, whatever the situation is. Can we work on taking control of ourselves? Can we promise ourselves that no external element (person or event) will control our happiness? I suggest that instead of saying "take care", we should practice saying "take charge."

We are so eager to take credit for the good things that happen in our lives that we use sentences like "I made the right decision at that time" or "I made a right investment that time." When things go wrong or do not happen the way we want, we blame it on other people or events, which most often means "it is not my fault." We might even ascribe it to fate and this certainly carries a negative connotation. If we are eager to take credit for all good things, we might as well have the courage to take responsibility for the bad things that happen as well.

Chapter 2

Achieve Your Goals

There is a story of an athlete who was running a marathon in an international event. When the race was over, the medals were presented to the winners and people started leaving the stadium. A press photographer was busy packing his bag to leave when he got a message on his pager that one athlete was still running. He decided to stay back till the runner arrived, anticipating a story for his paper. Quite a while later, he saw the athlete slowly limp into the stadium, do the last lap, cross the finishing line and collapse on the track. He ran up to him, gave him some water and helped him catch his breath. The photographer asked the athlete, "Why did you run? You knew that the race was over. You should have quit much earlier!" The athlete's reply: "My country sent me not to start the race, but to finish the race." Let us also commit ourselves to finish what we start, always!

Push Your Limits

When it comes to achieving things that we want in our lives, we impose limitations on ourselves. Much like a baby elephant that grows up chained to a tree continues to believe that it is still tied up even when the chain is simply around its legs and not bound to anything. It believes that it cannot walk as long as the chain is around its legs. We put such chains around our minds and tell ourselves that we cannot grow beyond a certain limit. We fail to see the immense potential lying untapped within ourselves and live a life that is mostly unfulfilled.

We are put on this earth to realise our full potential. We cannot limit ourselves by saying, "This is all I can do", "I do not have the skills to do it" or "I am not as good as others are." Stretch and reach out; see beyond what meets your eye.

When you closely observe successful people and those that are not as successful, you realise quite surprisingly that they use the same words when they approach tasks. The only difference is that those words are arranged in a different order. The latter would say, "It may be possible to succeed, but it is difficult." The former would say: "It may be difficult to succeed, but it is possible." The crux is to inculcate the possibility theory instead of the probability theory into our minds.

Get out of your comfort zone. Staying in it gives you some pleasure for some time. Getting out of it is almost always difficult. But the discomfort experienced when you are out of your comfort zone is only temporary. It might give you some pain, but it will also enable you to grow into a stronger person with richer experience. If the pupa decided to stay in the cocoon, we would never have seen a butterfly!

Spread The Love

Life can get difficult, but there are beautiful moments even in the midst of hardship. Here is something that happened a few years ago. I was waiting in the car for my wife to return from the fruit vendor, watching the evening traffic at a not-so-busy junction. I noticed the huddled figure of an old lady, sitting on the steps in front of some closed shops across the street. A few minutes later, an old man walked slowly towards her and sat down next to her. He opened a packet wrapped in a newspaper and took out a bun, broke it into two and gave her one piece. She searched the empty space in front of her before she could reach the bun; this told me she was blind. While they silently finished the bun, the man picked out another one from the packet and once more broke it into two, giving the lady one half. Again, they ate in silence.

Judging by his looks, the old man probably spent the whole day begging to buy them both something to eat. By this time, my wife was back and we drove home. I remained silent for a long time, leaving her to wonder what had happened to me. Even now, years later, a couple of questions linger in my mind. What could have been the old man's motivation to support her and feed her? Even in adverse conditions, how could he have an attitude of sharing? What could I learn from this? Think about this. Does the story wring your heart? There is so much love and respect in this world. Are we doing our best to spread the love?

In this age of terrorism and fanaticism, it can be difficult to think of spreading love and accepting or forgiving evildoers. More and more, we see an attitude of intolerance growing among people. "The weak can never forgive. Forgiveness is the attribute of the strong"—Mahatma Gandhi's words. In not forgiving, we declare to the world that we are weaklings. We also carry the burden of past, little hurts that were caused knowingly or unknowingly by others, those little defeats that we had to accept, those failures that we had to face, making our journey forward so difficult and slow. Forgiveness makes us feel relaxed and light. It shows strength of character. To make the journey of life comfortable, we have to learn to travel light.

Problems that we face can be classified into two—those with solutions and those without. The challenge is to find solutions for the ones in the first category. Many of us are problem-oriented instead of being solution-oriented. We focus too much on the problem and the more we do that, the bigger it gets. We have to deliberately shift focus to finding a solution instead and we might identify more than one solution for us to choose from.

Now consider the second category, the problems without solutions. In my opinion, these are not really problems. They are facts, which should be accepted to let life move on. Can we stop worrying about facts and start looking at solutions for problems? Let us move on in life.

Leave Your Mark

A long time ago, a ship docked in a port for operations. Once the work was over, the ship was preparing to set sail and the engine would not start. The engineers in the ship worked hard, but in vain. The agent of the ship in the port said that there was an automobile mechanic in that town who could repair any kind of engine and offered to call him. The captain agreed and the mechanic was called. The captain was shocked to see an old, haggard man walk in with just a hammer in his hand. Since he had no other option, the captain let him into the engine room. After looking around the engine room for a while, the mechanic moved into one corner of the engine room and gave a hard knock on a valve and asked for the engine to be started. To everyone's surprise, the engine roared into action. The old man silently walked away and the ship sailed. After a few days, the mechanic sent a bill for $1000 to the agent, who in turn sent it to the owners of the ship. The bill was rejected, saying it was way too high, and the owners wanted a break-up of the amount. The mechanic sent his break-up:

Cost of the knock: $1

Cost of knowing where to knock: $999

Knowledge is valuable. Engage in an unending pursuit of knowledge, and learn to apply it. Because "applied knowledge is power."

For everything that happens in our lives, we counter-act in one of the following ways: reflex, reaction or response. The fundamental difference between these is the time taken for the action. Reflex is almost always involuntary. Reaction is immediate. Response is a thought-out action. Reaction is most often knee-jerk and can prove to be wrong and unproductive. While I do not discount the fact that certain situations warrant immediate reaction, do we have the wisdom to avoid knee-jerk reactions and inculcate thought-out responses in our lives?

A few years ago, I read this in a book: "When the sun rises in the deepest forests of Africa, a lion wakes up and says to himself, 'Today I have to run faster than the slowest gazelle for me to survive.' At the same time, a gazelle wakes up and says to himself, 'Today I have to run faster than the fastest lion for me to survive.'" Every day, all of us have to run our races well in order to reach our destinations consistently. Whether in our personal lives, professional lives or in society, we should not be an "also ran" at the end of the race. Work hard to ensure that when we run, we give it all that we have. Can we be absolutely committed to the race that we are in? I bet our commitment can make this world a much better place!

Here is a story of another race: There once was a dog and a rabbit that lived in the same house. Whenever the rabbit came out of its burrow, the dog chased him. But the rabbit always managed to escape, getting back to the burrow without a scratch. After many days of disappointment and shame, the dog decided to befriend the rabbit. He went to the rabbit's burrow and called out to him. The rabbit refused to come out as he was not sure of the dog's intentions, telling the dog that he preferred to be inside. The dog said, "Hey, I am stronger and bigger than you, but how is it that you always win the race?" The rabbit replied, "My dear friend, while you were running for your lunch, I was running for my life!" I think this is true about our races too. What are we running for? Do we run for lunch or life?

Sometimes, we need a wake-up call in life. It was almost 8 o' clock and Tommy was still sleeping. His mother was upset since it was Monday and Tommy had to go to school. She tried waking him up several times, but in vain. When his mother's insistence increased, he sat up and told his mother that he hated to go to school because he had seen groups of students and even teachers in the campus gathered together to tease and ridicule him. He told her that he had noticed this several times and did not quite like it. Tommy's mother tried to console him and insisted that he go to school. Desperate as he was, he asked his mother to give one good reason for him to go school. His mother calmly replied, "Tommy, you have to go because you are the principal of the school." Many a time, we have to be reminded of who we are and what our roles in life are! We tend to forget and overlook, which results in confusion and chaos. Let us make an effort to internalise who we really are and start living our lives fully.

Faith is believing that when you put your foot forward there will be a floor under your feet or you will be given wings to fly. Faith is believing in something much before it happens. It is the unconditional acceptance that what you set out to do has already happened. It does not ask questions like "can I do it" or "do I have the ability." It is the foundation on which every edifice of success is built; a foundation that is first built in your mind before it is built in reality. It requires you to take stock of your strengths. Faith is believing in yourself so that one day the rest of the world believes you.

"Once you say a sentence, then you don't have the right to interpret it." This is one of the most powerful sentences that I have come across. If only all of us understood the meaning behind it, the world would have been a much better place. Once something has been said, it is for the person who listens to interpret it. Thus, the responsibility of the speaker is to say it in such a way that the listener gets the same meaning as that intended by the speaker. Here is a wonderful story. A very fat lady, while coming out of a shop, saw a beggar standing by the road. The beggar told the lady, "Madam, I have not eaten for three days." The lady looked at him and exclaimed, "I wish I had your will power." Have a hearty laugh, but please do not miss the message!

It is important to step into others' shoes every once in a while. An old man was taking a walk on a beach one evening when he saw hundreds of starfish washed ashore by the waves. He knew that if they were not in water, they would not survive. He started picking them up one by one and throwing them back into the sea. A young man who was jogging by saw this and told the old man, "I think you are wasting your time. There are hundreds of them. It will not make a difference." The old man bent down, picked up one starfish, threw it into the sea and told the young man, "It made a world of a difference to that one." We all can make a difference to at least one human being with our words and deeds. Let us promise that we will do our best to make a difference!

Managing Expectations, Managing Life

It takes a lot of effort to make a relationship work and make it last a lifetime. In my opinion, the most important factor in making a relationship work is managing expectations. To do that, one has to know what the other is expecting from him/her. This holds true in all kinds of relationships, be it professional or personal. Many a time, friction arises in a relationship when expectations are not met because they are not communicated with each other. We tend not to talk about it and yet expect the other to fulfil those expectations. We feel bad when that does not happen and often it is because they do not know what is expected. Let us pack some openness into ourselves and learn to communicate our expectations in all our relationships; start with family.

Values and morals are passed down in families, often through generations. While addressing a group of primary school children, a trainer asked them about traffic signals. He asked them the meaning of red and green signals, to which they gave correct answers. He then asked them, “What are you supposed to do when you see a yellow light?” Almost all the children shouted in unison, “Speed up and cross the junction!” How would they know this? They have obviously seen elders around them do this at traffic junctions. Likewise, if we have to teach children values in life, we have to make a conscious effort to demonstrate it to them. Our words and deeds have to be in sync. Let us teach our children strong value systems on which they can build their lives.

Talking of traffic, it pains and angers me to see the blatant defiance and denial of rules on the road. I am concerned not because the drivers do not comply, but because they are teaching the young generation that it is ok to break the rules. A father on a bike, with his child sitting in front and the mother of the child riding pillion, rides against oncoming traffic, on the wrong side of the road at a busy junction, while talking on a mobile phone stuck in his helmet. An autorickshaw, carrying students more than its capacity, zigzagging its way in busy traffic, with the driver showering abuses on people who do not move when he honks. A cyclist, riding alongside the median, on a four-lane road, tries to race motor vehicles. A driver at a traffic signal honking his way to heaven, believing that his horn is connected to the accelerator of the vehicle in front.

Can we instil sense into at least one driver a week and inspire him to comply? Can we ask the auto driver who takes us from point A to point B not to squeeze his way through busy traffic? Can we consciously teach the younger generation that their lives are not to be wasted under bus or truck wheels? Can we work on not turning roads into racetracks? I believe we can!

Resilience is the ability of an object to return to its original shape after it has been stretched or compressed. In human beings, it refers to the inner strength to bounce back from a setback, or the ability to adapt to adverse conditions in life. Life does not always dish out the sweetest of dishes. Many a time, we will be served a portion of bitter or sour dishes, catapulting us into a state of shock and disbelief. The speed with which we can bounce back and move on with life determines our future. We will bounce back if we believe in our hearts that "this too shall pass." Yes, both good times and bad times do not last long. By becoming resilient people, we can convert those sharp turns on the road of life into smooth curves.

"Tenacity" is a word I cannot get enough of. It is defined as "the quality of being determined to do or achieve something." It talks about the "firmness of purpose." That brings me to a very important question: What is the purpose of life? It is very critical that we identify our life-purpose so that we can work with determination to achieve it. Being without a defined purpose would make us "wandering generality", which means we just float like driftwood. Having a purpose would, however, make us part of a smaller group called "meaningful specifics", who know where they are going and what they want to achieve by the time they are done with their lives. Firmness of purpose will add meaning to our mornings, quality to our days and hope to our evenings.

Time management is one of those important productive habits the experts say we need to achieve success. Can we actually manage time? Whether we like it or not, the clock ticks on relentlessly. How do we manage something over which we have no control? Thus, more than managing time, we have to learn to manage our activities. On that point, most of us tend to attend to urgent things and overlook the important ones. It has even gotten into our vocabulary. For instance, "I have to urgently reach my client's office" or "I have an urgent meeting to attend." The important things that we put off will become urgent at some point of time. That is when panic strikes and we go crazy about lack of time, saying, "I am too busy." The key is to identify the important things that need to be done and prioritise them the previous day. You may initially have to carry some over to the next day, but over a period of time, you will master the art and will become a better time manager.

What if, despite your best attempts and after managing time effectively, you still stumble? It was some time back that I read this: "When you fall during the journey of life, make sure that you fall forward so that you are closer to your goal." I found this very profound. It is a given that we will fall. None of us have learned to walk without falling down. However, after a couple of falls, did we tell our parents that we are sick and tired of trying to walk? Did we tell them that it is very difficult and so we are quitting? Why do we then get scared of falling down? The point is, falling down is not abnormal and is not a sign of inability. It is normal and part of the learning curve. The crucial thing here is to get up after each fall. The mantra should be "one more time, one more time."

I was once called to do a training program for autorickshaw drivers, which was inaugurated by a senior police officer. In his address, he touched upon the various causes of road accidents. According to him, one of the major reasons for accidents was the fact that drivers were doing their job without the realisation that they are doing a "job." When they drove, their minds wandered and driving became purely mechanical. Their focus would be on everything except driving. Is this not the same challenge that most of us face? We do what we have to do for the sake of doing it. We too do not focus. We end up with unfinished work, heaps of frustration and depleted self-confidence. Remember the question Arjuna was asked by Dronacharya pointing at the target hung from a tree? "What do you see?" If we see the target and only the target, we win.

I am sure you have heard the story of the balloon man. To announce his arrival at a village, the balloon seller would fill balloons with helium and let them soar into the sky. Seeing them, children flocked around him to buy balloons in different colours. An African-American boy, watching all this from behind a tree, walked up to him and asked, "Sir, can you fly a black balloon?" The balloon man filled a black balloon with helium and let it go up. Looking at the flying balloon he said, "My dear child, it is not the colour of the balloon that makes it fly. It is what is inside that makes it fly." How true about our lives too! It is what is inside of us that will take us places; our character and values will fly us to great heights in life.

There is a story of a father who came back very tired after a hectic day in office and wanted to rest for a while. He sat on the couch with a magazine and a cup of coffee. However, his 5-year-old son wanted to play with him and kept pulling at his trousers asking him to play. The father kept avoiding him, but the little boy's insistence grew to a point of irritation. In order to keep him occupied for a while, the father tore off a page from the magazine which had the world map on it, tore it into small bits and gave it to the child asking him to put the map together again. The father let out a sigh of relief as the child got busy with the task. In five minutes, the child came back having completed the task. The father was astonished and asked him how he could do it so fast. He never thought the 5-year-old could put together a world map. The child replied with a smile, "On the other side of the page was the face of a man. When I put the man together, the world kind of came together!" Try not to correct the world, but work hard to correct yourself; as a result, the world will get corrected!

In computer jargon, there is a term GIGO, which expands to "garbage in, garbage out." This principle is applicable to the most powerful computer on earth too—the human mind. If misinformation or junk is fed into the computer, the output generated by the system also would be junk. One does not have to be a rocket scientist to understand this fact. Likewise, the mind, if fed nonsensical information, would certainly produce useless output. Now, think about the input that is being fed into our minds. All kinds of crime-related news from the media or negative thoughts about one's own profession related to work pressure, inadequate compensation or stress created due to financial difficulties are essentially negative input. The mind processes such information and brings out even more negative thoughts, which prove harmful to our own existence. Can we deliberately attempt to ward off negative inputs, so that the output always remains positive? I believe we can deliberately work on providing positive input to the mind so that it can counter-balance the effect of negativity that goes in without our permission.

It is true that technology has made our lives easier, brought faraway places closer, and improved the quality of our lives as well as kept us updated about developments across the world. Take the mobile phone, though. While it has brought a lot of convenience, it has taken away a lot of other important things from us. Let me give you an example: When I travelled alone during my student days, I used to savour nature through the window of the bus or train. I enjoyed the wind and loved the raindrops on my face. I looked at billboards of shops and learned names of new places. I am sure those of you who went to school and college in the 1980s would have done the same thing. Now however, I see people plugged into their mobile phones, either listening to music, speaking to someone or watching a movie. They do not see the world around them. I ask myself, "Are they not missing something? Do they know that there is a world outside the mobile phone?" I think we should learn to ask "May I call you later?" I believe these kinds of gadgets are there for us to use and not for the gadgets to use us.

Find Your Potential

There is the story of a donkey that fell into an unused well in a village. Since the well was too deep for it to jump out and escape, it started crying out loud, hoping for help. After some time, the people heard its cry and came running to the well. They tried to get the donkey out by employing different methods, but in vain. Finally, after many hours of toil, the villagers decided to give up and let the donkey die. They also felt that the well would never be used again and so decided to fill it up. They brought soil from elsewhere and started to put into the well. The poor donkey was going to be buried alive, but it did not understand what was going on. One after the other, piles of soil started falling on its body. Each time soil fell on its body, out of sheer anger it shook its body, to get the soil off. Quite a while later, it realised that it was standing on a huge pile of soil and was very close to the opening of the well. It then jumped out and ran away to freedom. Similarly, when life throws piles of desperation, failure and bad experiences at us, can we, like the donkey, learn to shake it off? Can we learn to stand on top of it all and declare that we will never be buried alive?

It was some years ago that I read this beautiful sentence: "Any one can count the number of seeds in an apple, but only God can count the number of apples in a seed." There could not be a better way to express the innate potential of every individual. We are all seeds that can produce an infinite number of apples. We may not have looked inside us and so would have been thinking "What can I do?" There is so much latent ability in all of us that can be tapped into, which would trigger possibilities leading to great things. The key is to unlock our inner capabilities. I challenge you to spend some time everyday to identify your inner strengths. You would be surprised to know that you are so powerful and unique.

Success—most of you would associate the word with money. What do we know to do with money? I guess a majority would answer, "Spend, what else?" Like everything in life, we learned this from our parents. Most of us, during our childhood, have seen the panic and stress on the faces of our parents as they near the end of the month. Instead of "money left at the end of the month", it was a lot of "month left at the end of the money." Eventually, when it comes to some emergency, we turn to friends or banks for loans, which increases the burden.

The equation which many of us follow as far as money goes is: Income – Expenses = Savings. And in most of our cases, the right side of the equation is always zero or negative. There is a simple way out of this—

change the equation! Income – Savings = Expenses. Spend only after saving a pre-determined amount from your income.

Above all, do not despair or give up. The other day, a local news channel carried the story of three students who were awaiting their Class 10 examination results. The common thread among the three was that they all went through severe adversities during their examinations. One of the stories touched me and reinforced my belief that it is the strength of your purpose or goal that drives you. It was about a girl who lost her father a day before one of the exams. Nevertheless, she prepared for the exam and wrote it well. After finishing the exam, she went to the cemetery to attend her father's funeral service. In an interview, she said that she was confident that she would score very high marks. I will never be able to comprehend the depths of her sorrow nor will I ever understand how she went through the ordeal. But I know that she had no other option but to appear for the exam and face life boldly, mainly so that she can support her mother and siblings in future. Determination moves mountains!

Chapter 3

Living for Others: Giving Back to Society

We speak of "give and take." Have you wondered why the phrase is not "take and give"? Simply because you are supposed to give before you take! The act of giving is not restricted to money—you can give your time, care or even smile to others. Compliment those around you for something that they have done. You might turn their day around. What you give will be returned in abundant measure when you need it the most. Inculcate an attitude of generosity; never waste an opportunity to give!

We should though, understand the difference between giving and sacrificing. The dictionary meaning of "giving" says: "Freely transfer the possession of something to someone." That is, you act on your free will without expecting anything in return. "Sacrifice" means: "Forfeiture of something highly valued for the sake of one considered to have a greater value or claim." In my understanding, there is an element of expectation in sacrifice, as also a tinge of pain. To explain further, ideally you would not want to give up that something because you consider it very dear, but are willing to sacrifice. That is when the pain kicks in. But when you give, you give it with happiness, contentment and without pain; you not only transfer something, but also our happiness to someone!

An interesting story is told of a hen and a pig, who were close friends, walking on the road one day. While passing a church, they saw a board put up that read "donations are accepted for the poor." On discussing the subject, both felt that they should donate something. As they were contemplating what to donate, the hen asked, "Why don't we donate eggs and bacon?" The pig thought for a while and replied, "For you it is a donation, but for me it is total commitment!" While the hen has to only lay an egg, the pig has to sacrifice its life. The key word here is commitment and without it you will get nowhere. Commitment calls for unwavering focus, untiring effort and an excellent attitude. The best part about being committed is that whatever you are working on will get better by the day.

Generosity comes with empathy, that deep emotional understanding of another person's problems and viewpoints. During a training session, the trainer asked participants to exchange their footwear for their neighbour's. He then asked the participants to share what they felt about wearing somebody else's shoes.

Almost everyone said that it felt uncomfortable. The trainer said, "Being in another's shoes is always uncomfortable. And that is empathy." Keep this in mind when you are at the receiving end of unacceptable behaviour from other people. Be comforted by the thought that probably, with their background, that is the best they could say or do. Remember this also when you come across the underprivileged. Have a big heart to comfort them in whatever small way you can. Empathy is the forerunner of compassion and when these emotions come together, great things can happen.

Take a moment to think of how much time we spend daily on what we consider important things. We spend time in offices, with our loved ones, on activities like shopping or parties and on health, among others. When do we spend time with ourselves? I do not think we do. I ask you to look at allocating some time of the day to spend with just yourself.

There is much that you can do alone, for yourself. Some introspection, some pampering, some reading. You will be pleasantly surprised to note that you can be at peace with yourself; you will be more relaxed. You might find time to do some silly things, which may make you laugh like you never have before. Eventually, you will find that you are more efficient at work and that your relationships have more meaning and dimensions. So try and incorporate a little me-time in your daily routine.

As far as success and achieving things in life are concerned, the thumb rule is, "You can either like the method or you can like the results." We all want good health, but do not like to get up early and exercise. We like having money but do not like to work hard with focus. We like promotions, but do not like to put anything extra into our work. Every good and enjoyable result is preceded by a not-so-enjoyable process. Unless we go through that process, we will not have the result that we wish for. Focus on the result and carry on—you will eventually start enjoying the method too. You will soon be well on your way to success.

There were two neighbouring villages where the rain gods were not so kind. The practice among these villagers was to pray for rain whenever drought hit them. They sang and danced to please the gods. Despite all the prayers, it rained only in one village. The inhabitants of the other village wondered how their neighbours were blessed with rain. They decided to go to the chief of the village where it rained to ask him what their secret was. The chief said, "We dance until it rains." The drought-hit villagers understood why they never had any rain—they sang and danced and then waited for rain, while their neighbours continued dancing till it rained. My interpretation of this is that all of us have to keep working until we achieve our goals. Never stop working after sometime and then wait for the result; work until you see the result. The mantra should be "I will, until."

WHAT WE ARE
LEAP OF FAITH
WHAT WE WAN TO BE
MAKE THE JUMP.

Chapter 4

Faith: Believing before Receiving

The wheel of life has five spokes, the five Fs—family, friends, finance, faith and fitness. If any of these spokes were out of alignment, the wheel would wobble. All these areas are to be given equal importance and should be well aligned for life to roll smoothly. A vast majority of us give less importance and priority to one or two areas and this is when the wheel gets thrown off balance. It is very critical that work hard for that balance and maintain it.

Have faith that good things will come. When you ask for something that you want badly, you have to believe that you have received it before physically receiving it. There is a story about a group of people who were going to the top of a mountain to pray to God for blessing their village with abundant rain. Among them was a little boy carrying an umbrella, the only one who had thought of taking one along. People with him asked why he was carrying an umbrella, to which he replied that as they were going to pray for rain, he thought he should be prepared for rain. What an excellent manifestation of faith! God will never deny that kind of faith. He has no option but to give you what you ask for!

Another tale is told of two Buddhist monks. On their way back to the monastery, they came across a beautiful lady in a long white dress standing by the road. She stood near a puddle of dirty water and mud, looking worried and confused. The older monk asked her what the matter was. She said that she had to go back to her house, but could not find a way to cross the puddle of mud, which, she was afraid, would dirty her beautiful dress. On hearing this, the older monk lifted her in his arms, carried her across the puddle and put her down requesting her to proceed to her house. The monks continued towards the monastery. The younger monk was a little perplexed. He was not sure if what his senior did was right. Unable to contain his curiosity, he voiced his concern to the senior. "Don't you know that touching a lady is forbidden? You have now carried one. Is it not a grave mistake?" The older one replied, "My friend, I carried and left her by the side of that puddle. Why are you still carrying her?"

Like the young monk, all of us carry unwanted thoughts, for no reason at all. It is these thoughts that reduce the speed of our journey considerably. Travel light, travel fast. That too, with peace of mind.

"There is more hunger in the world for love and appreciation than for bread"—these are the immortal words of Mother Teresa. According to my mentor, we must learn to compliment people on something always. But what we see around us is just the opposite. We are too miserly when it comes to appreciating others. Simple words of appreciation can trigger greater achievements. This applies more in the case of children. They are sure to be propelled to greater heights of performance in their studies and further, with our appreciation and love acting as rocket boosters. But keep your compliments genuine and heartfelt and avoid shallow praise.

Mahatma Gandhi once said, "Strength does not come from physical capacity. It comes from an indomitable will." And he is one man who proved it right by rewriting the course of history. Winning is not a function of the size of the man in the fight, but a function of the size of the fight in the man. The will to win produces enough strength, which stays with each one of us with a never-say-die attitude. It generates tremendous power and unstoppable action, resulting in sure-shot achievement of the goals that we set for ourselves. The secret for creating this kind of will is to free the mind from the pains of going through a fight. Allow the mind focus on enjoying the victory or the result. As you know, where there is a will, there is a way.

I read this sentence a long time ago: "Every sinner has a future and every saint has a past." I would like to read this thus: "Your past has no bearing on your future, and so the future can be entirely different from what your past was." In statistics and economics, trend analysis and extrapolation might help predict quantitatively measurable indicators. But I believe a radical change is possible overnight, more so in the case of human beings. All you need is to make a decision. The most challenging part is the process of making a decision. But once that is done, you are good to go! Let us learn to make strong decisions.

Most of us feel lost when it comes to long-term planning. We are inclined to think that it is impossible to see beyond a couple of years and hence refrain from making long-term commitments. Imagine you are travelling to a destination about 300 km away and you are driving at night. The headlights of your car reach up to only 50 m or so. You will still reach your destination with a visual range of just 50 m at a time. Break your long-term plans and goals into short-term finishing points. These finishing points are well within your sight and thus you will be able to reach them without getting scared. Bit by bit, you would have conquered your long-term goal even before you realise it. To keep your spirits up, you could reward yourself when you reach such finishing points and gear up for the next lap.

If you were asked to choose between good, better and best, what would you choose? The answer seems obvious. But here is a different perspective. There is only one "best" and there is nothing beyond that. But "better" gives you room for further advancement. You strive to be better than the previous, whatever it might be. For example, your today can be made better than yesterday. It also means there is no limit to the process of improvement. The Japanese call this "kaizen." Can we work hard to be better in every walk of life that we are involved in? Yes, we can!

I believe there are three dimensions to goodness in life. The first one is to do good. You do not have to wait for a right time; do good to others in whatever small way you can. The second dimension is to feel good. You have to feel good about yourself, about others and about everything that comes across your life. It makes you feel light and free. The third dimension is being good. It should be second nature to you. When that is the case, you will not need to make an effort to do good and feel good; those will come naturally.

Martin Luther King once said, "Our scientific power has outrun our spiritual power. We have guided missiles and misguided men." We have made very significant advances in the field of science, so much so that we virtually have everything at our fingertips. We can steer spaceships from earth stations, launch missiles across the globe, track somebody who is travelling in a car and drop a bomb. But what is happening to our conscience? What about our values? We need to put in a concerted effort to get ourselves onto the right track so that we treat others as human beings. We have a responsibility to see that our children are shown the path of justice and mutual respect.

There was once an adventure-loving person, who used to try extremely dangerous stunts. He once decided to cross the Niagara Falls on a tightrope. He began preparing himself by walking on a tightrope tied at a certain height on land. As he perfected his art, he kept increasing the height at which the rope was tied. The news of his grand plan spread far and wide and people began to swarm the place where he was practising. A young press reporter, after having watched the man for a few days, walked up to him and said, "I have been watching you for some days now. I believe you are now ready to cross the waterfalls." The man looked at her and asked, "Do you really believe so?" "Yes, I believe", she replied. The man then asked her, "If that is so, why don't I do it tomorrow, and let me carry you on my shoulder as I walk across the falls?" Needless to say, the lady disappeared from the scene. Belief can never be so shallow, it has to be deep, very, very deep.

"I will do today what others won't, so that I can live tomorrow like others can't." Is it not a powerful sentence? Many of us wonder why we are not living a life that we wanted. To me, the answer is simple. We are not doing things that would get us the life that we want. It is much like saying "I want a flat tummy" and not doing things that would get you one. You do not like your potbelly, but are you willing to get up and sweat it out every day? Yes, every day! Most of you will not. So you keep the belly. Is life any different from this example? You need to go through the process to get to your goal.

Conclusion

"A small body of determined spirits fired by an unquenchable faith in their mission can alter the course of history." Powerful words from Mahatma Gandhi. Though we understand the meaning and relevance of this sentence, let us look at it from an analytical angle. He first talks about "small body"—not nation, not entire state, but "small body." The number just does not matter. He then talks about "determined spirits"—unstoppable people who will never lose focus on what they set out to do. He continues to "unquenchable faith." Unwavering faith in oneself and faith in the mission to be accomplished are elements that fire action in you. No one can talk such people out of their goal. He concludes with "alter the course of history." There are many who just live and die. But some want to be a part of history. They want to leave a name behind. I strongly believe you have it in you to be a part of this group. Are you game?

It is often said, "a good life is the enemy of a great life." I sometimes feel that the reason many of us do not put in our best to do something is the above statement. Many of us have all the ingredients of a good life—a house, vehicle, good food and so on. However, it might help us, and the people around us, if we ask ourselves the question, "Is this the best that I can do?" This will throw up opportunities and untapped capabilities lying dormant within us. You will find yourself recharged for action, because you deserve not just life, but a great life.

By complying with some basic norms and spending some time in retrospect, we can all do a mid-course correction on life. It is my firm belief that every reader will find this book a useful tool and that I have been able to stir your thoughts through this medium. As you read, join me on this journey and pen your thoughts. This way, we can explore together the ways of better living with effective communication that would benefit all. Let each of us begin by complying and co-existing with everyone we meet today and as we spread our ideas of peaceful living, let us build a happier and more harmonious community around us to Level Next.

Learning Notes